Little Things

Olamma Maji

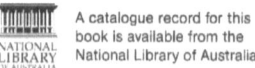
A catalogue record for this book is available from the National Library of Australia

Copyright © 2023 Olamma Maji
All rights reserved.
ISBN: 978-1-922727-88-6

Linellen Press
265 Boomerang Road
Oldbury, Western Australia
www.linellenpress.com.au

Dedication

I would like to appreciate the Almighty God, the giver of life, strength and wisdom, who makes all things possible. I thank my beloved husband apostle Isaiah Maji for his words of wisdom and encouragement. I appreciate my children and everyone who supported or supports me one way or another in my daily life.

I am grateful, God, bless you greatly.

Contents

Little Things i

Dedication iii

Contents v

Chapter One 1

Chapter Two 9

Chapter Three 20

Chapter Four 27

Chapter Five 37

About the Author 44

Chapter One

It Does Not Make Sense

Most times in life people only see the big picture: when you look at a photograph, do you see the person or the image? What about what makes up the image, which are the lines and the dots? It may only take people who are artistic to notice that or they may not even notice it at all. But without the lines and the dots, the image will never be formed.

In the movie industry, people, society or the world only see and notice the actor or actress and celebrate them; they cannot go out into public areas without people requesting an autograph, without people screaming and wanting a piece of them. Nobody notices or knows the make-up artist, the producer, the director, the cleaner, the cook, the photographer, the customers and so on

In an organisation, people celebrate the manager, and the directors when things are working, but the cleaner may never be noticed. In church, people see or notice the preacher, the choir, the ushers, but there are also some who may not be noticed – the cleaners, or anyone who cleans both in secret and in the open. Nobody notices the one who prays for the church; the one who does secret evangelism; the one whose acts or actions make people ask, 'Where do you worship?' They come to your church because of your behaviour, because of your enthusiasm towards God. They know you are different and everything about you is different; they just want to be part of that uniqueness.

There was a church where the move of God was so evident: people were getting healed, miracles were everywhere … until suddenly things became still. It looked like nothing was happening anymore. The pastor was surprised and wondering what had happened. He received a revelation that the old woman who was always praying for the church had died and no one was praying.

So the man remembered there was an old woman who sat at the back of the church; she was always there and always consistent but no one noticed her. Who could believe that? The woman who looked frail and fragile could control so much.

Thank You and Sorry

A little word such as 'I am sorry' and 'thank you' go a long way. Instead of prolonging an argument or looking for who to apportion blame, a little word such as I am sorry can melt the heart of anyone.

Proverbs 15:1 says *a soft answer turns away wrath.* The emphasis is on 'soft', which means the words are gentle and calm. Someone can be so upset, full of fire, and look like they could pull down a building, a little word such as 'I am sorry' could calm the person. In the parable of the leper in Luke 17, it was only one man who came back to say thank you after they had received their healing and this act melted Jesus' heart. He told the leper he was made whole.

Luke 17: 11 *Now it happened as he went to Jerusalem that he passed through the midst of Samaria and Galilee. Then as he entered a certain village they met him ten men who were lepers who stood afar off and they lifted up their voices and said "Jesus, Master have mercy on us!" So when he saw them, he said to them, "Go, show yourself to the priest." And so it was that as they went, they were cleansed and one of them when he saw that he was healed, returned with a loud voice glorified God and fell down on his feet giving him thanks. So Jesus answered and said "Were there not ten cleansed? But where are the nine? Were there not any found who returned to give glory to God except this foreigner?"*

Jesus is our example when it comes to gratitude. He gave thanks whenever he prayed. For example: in the story of Lazarus:

.. .. and Jesus lifted up his eyes and said "Father, I thank you that you have heard me and I know you always hear me." John 11; 41 and 42.

This is the story of Lazarus who had died and was in the grave for four days. Jesus prayed. After he thanked God, he commanded Lazarus to come out of the grave and he rose up from the grave. John 11: 1 to 44. Jesus thanked the Father for all he had been doing for him, and also thanked him in advance for answered prayers because he had faith that God had done it.

'Thank you' may only be two words but they are powerful. They are the expression of gratitude; it will make you and the person you are saying it to feel happy. It is a fuel for more action. It opens doors. It may be small but it changes things. A word as little as 'thank you' and 'I am sorry' can make people become enemies or friends for life. It's a show of respect and love.

Act of Kindness

Abigail was a woman of great understanding and very beautiful. Her husband's name was Nabal; he was very rich, harsh and evil in his doings. One day, as was the custom in those days, he decided to share some of his sheep with his shepherd. A great man named David sent his men to Nabal requesting whatever Nabal could offer him and his men. David told his men to remind Nabal that he and his men had protected Nabal's servants and watched over them, preventing enemies from attacking them and not harming them. Nabal treated David's men harshly and refused to give them anything.

David's men went back and told him what Nabal had said. David was upset and started organising men to fight Nabal and his men. Nabal's wife Abigail heard the plot and arranged some gifts with some of her servants, and they went quickly to intercept David and his men on their way. She begged him on behalf of her husband, and offered the gift to David and pleaded with him to forgive her husband. David considered her plead and act of kindness and did not attack her household.

Though David showed an act of kindness to Nabal's servant when they were at a place called Carmel, Nabal did not reciprocate the act of kindness which could have led to war. Another act of kindness from his wife Abigail changed the turn of events. (1 Samuel 25)

*****

Rehab was a prostitute who saved two spies from being killed in Jericho. Let me tell you a little about the story.

The children of Israel were slaves in Egypt for many years. God sent a deliverer to them in the way of Moses; Moses led the children of Israel out of Egypt. God had promised them he would give them Canaan, so, on their way, Joshua sent two spies to spy on the land of Jericho. Two of the spies went to a lady called Rehab who was a prostitute. The king of Jericho, knowing their presence and their mission, wanted them, but Rehab hid them and allowed them to escape through her roof. She told the spies to remember her and show her household mercy when they eventually destroyed or captured Jericho.

(Joshua 2 : 12: *Now therefore I beg you, swear to me by the Lord since I have shown you kindness that you also will show kindness to my father's house and give me a true token.*

When Israel was finally captured and Jericho destroyed, only Rehab and her household were spared because of her kindness to the spies.

Do not be deceived whatsoever: a man sows that he shall reap.

An act of kindness from Rehab spared her generation. She was the great-great-grandmother of King David. She is part of Jesus' family tree. Who would have thought that, of all the people that would be saved, one would be a prostitute. For God does not think as men think.

It is often said that 'one good turn deserves another'. Being kind to people does not really take much effort, but some people see it as a weakness or as being weak or fear being taken advantage of.

Chapter Two

The Beginning Stage

The beginning stage of things sometimes does not really make sense. When you see an artist trying to draw, you might wonder what they are doing – the skeletal representation of their work is unexplainable – it looks like rubbish – but the more the artist continues, the more the work takes form until you get a masterpiece that people will pay millions of dollars for.

In the creation story in Genesis chapter one, the earth was without form and void. Darkness was upon the face of the deep. Try imagining this: see the world without the houses, the cars, the humans, the animals and everything else there is. See the world as empty, shapeless and without form. So difficult to imagine, isn't it?

But the earth was once empty. Who could have thought that something that was so empty, so deformed, so shapeless and lifeless could be filled with so much that some wicked people feel others (or weaker ones) should be eliminated so there will not be population-explosion.

Something that was so empty is now so full.

God saw the potential in something that was nameless and formless and he said 'let there be light and there was light'; when he saw the prospect, he continued; he did not stop at the light; he went further like the artist. He created the heavens. This was the second day. On the third day He created dry ground and plants. He knew it could be better; He could see hope and a future with the world. He created the sun, moon and stars, birds and sea animals. It takes vision, and determination to continue. He decided to make land animals, including humans. After he created these beautiful things, he decided to rest on the 7th day. Even though the world was nothing, He could see something in nothing. God did not give up on it; He was patient, consistent and dedicated to his work to make sure everything came out perfect.

The foundation of a building does not really look good when you see where a foundation is being laid; it looks like they are destroying the ground. You see bits and pieces everywhere; it looks like they are putting wood together; it does not really make sense but it is the structural base that stands on the ground and supports the building. Someone can easily give up on the foundation if they don't know or understand what you are building because it does not really make sense.

From something that does not make sense comes this beautiful structure that people pay thousands of dollars for. People live in it and are protected from the harshness of the weather. This great mansion actually came from an ideal; sometimes an ideal is just a dot or a line that does not make sense but from it comes this beautiful creation. All the builder needs is the idea, the vision, the patience and the determination to finish. But the thing is, it is not everyone that sees the finishing from the beginning; some people see the foundation and think it will never be a masterpiece; some have the idea but never start the foundation because they cannot see the finishing; some can see the finishing but they don't have the patience and determination to continue.

However, like the butterfly, do not despise the days of little beginnings. In the metamorphosis of a butterfly, the young butterfly is very different from the adult. It starts with an egg, which changes to larvae, then pupa and adult. The transformation is amazing because every stage completely looks different. Who could tell that the ugly larvae could become such a beautiful butterfly?

Are There Really Little Things and Who Notices It?

(Joshua 2 : 12: *Now therefore I beg you, swear to me by the Lord since I have shown you kindness that you also will show kindness to my father's house and give me a true token.*

Zachariah 4:10 says: *Do not despise the days of small things.*

Great things come from little things. Jesus said in Mathew 21:42 the stone which the builder rejected has become the chief cornerstone. This is the Lord's doing and it is marvelous in our eyes. The stone was considered useless, rejected, forsaken, not qualified, not able, not good enough, not strong enough, because the builder did not see the potential of the stone. He decided to reject it, to dump it, throw it in a corner. That same stone became celebrated, in charge; became the landlord of the corner. Other stones looked up to the stone for advice and encouragement because it understood what it meant to be a castaway.

Foolish Things

1 Corinthians 1:27 to 28: *But God has chosen the foolish things of the world to put to shame the wise and God has chosen the weak things of the world to put to shame the things which are mighty. And the base things of the world and the things which are despised God has chosen and the things which are not to bring to nothing the things that are.*

God is still in the business of taking people from nothing and making them something. Sometimes, people may look at you and make conclusions about you; they may think it is over for you; they may think you will die as nothing. They may think you will never stop that bad habit; they may think you will never end well.

They may think God will never show you mercy – to them, you went too far, whatever you did. They think it is unforgivable; they think hell is the only option for you.

There is a story of a man who had gone too far in black magic; he had literally sacrificed all the members of his family to acquire and sustain his wealth. He sacrificed every year one member of his family for ten years. When there were no more loved family members to use, his life had to go. To sacrifice himself was the only option.

But he loved himself too much and did not want to kill himself. The evil powers tormented him day and night and were not willing to let him go. So, he ran to the church, confessed what he had done and surrendered his life to Jesus.

To you and I, we may say he deserved to die for all the killings he had done. We may say he deserved to rot in hell. But that was not the case for this man, because God forgave him.

The man became a preacher, winning souls for God and exposing the kingdom of darkness and their operation. It may not make sense that God would use such a person, but he did and he still does.

From the Bush to the Palace

David in the bible started little. He was taking care of his father's sheep in the bush, singing and playing his instrument to the animals. He was dedicated. No one knew him. He was a young man that no one noticed, busy doing his thing in the bush. But God noticed him and when it was time for promotion, election, elevation, God chose him to be the king of Israel. Even though his brothers, who were more qualified, were presented to Samul to be anointed as king, God did not choose them.

David's brothers fought battles for the country and everyone knew them as warriors; they represented the family in times of war. David was in his corner doing his thing. No one noticed him. It looked like what he was doing was not a big deal. I am sure in the eyes of his brothers they would have considered him weak, a small boy, a daddy's boy.

David took food to his brothers at the war camp during the time of war between Israel and the Philistines in the time of Goliath.

1 Samuel 17: 17: … *then Jesse said to his son David, take now for your brothers an ephah of this dried grain and this ten loaves and run to your brothers at the camp*

He ran errands for his father which were not a prestigious act especially for a man, but he was happy doing his thing in his corner till God located and placed him above all his family, made him a king and a ruler over Israel.

The Slave Girl

The slave girl in 2 Kings Chapter 5, from verse one, though the bible did not say her name, she was inconsequential; she was at her lowest. There was nothing worse than being a slave but she was instrumental to the healing of Naaman.

Let me narrate the story to you.

The slave girl, as the bible calls her, was captured by the Syrian Army during the war in Israel. She was assigned to wait on Naaman's wife – Naaman was the commander of the Syrian Army, but he was a leper. The slave girl advised Naaman's wife for her husband to go to Israel and meet with prophet Elisha to receive his healing. Her mistress listened to her advice, even though she was a slave. Naaman went to Israel and received his healing.

Supposing Naaman or his wife disregarded her: Naaman would have died as a leper. But the reverse happened in this case. Sometimes greatness comes in small packages.

In life, you can't afford to look down on anyone because the time you disregard, disrespect and treat someone unfairly may be when God has decided to bless them. Treat people with respect no matter who they are because, in the sight of God, no one is useless. No one is inconsequential. No one is a mistake. After all, the world was void, deformed and shapeless but he still used it.

Jesus told his disciples in Act1:8:

But you shall receive power when the holy spirit has come upon you and you shall be witness to me in Jerusalem, in all Judea and Samaria and to the end of the Earth.

That means it is okay to start small – there is room for growth. God may recognise small, but he does not see you as small. Start somewhere; start something, for a little drop of water makes a mighty ocean.

Job 8;7 says, though your beginning was small, yet your latter end will increase abundantly. There is always room for increase.

Chapter Three

The Abuse

Her life was a mess. She constantly thought of what she went through as a child – the rape by her stepfather from six years old until she was fourteen. She never told anyone, not even her mother because she felt no one would believe her. She lived a sad and depressed life; she hated not just men but everyone around her.

She married twice and divorced twice because she was trying to fill the void she felt. She was a bitter person and, as it is said, you cannot give what you do not have – she did not have love and she did not know how to receive love.

At thirty-eight, it dawned on her that she was getting older and her life was gradually passing before her eyes. She knew she could fool the world but could not fool herself.

"My world is sad," she said, "and I don't want anyone to go through what am going through." She finally decided to speak out, and went for counselling for the first time in her life; she finally told someone what she went through as a child and how she was feeling.

By going to therapy, she began to heal. The more she spoke about it, the better she felt. She went public and received so many calls because lots of people could relate to her. They were able to open up to her. She took a course in counselling and finally found her purpose as she surrendered to God and became the strength to many.

There are many stories like this about people who went through physical, sexual and mental abuse as children. Their life was one of pain and tears but the Lord still used them. It's not about the beginning. It is the end that matters.

The Truth about Thought

You may feel like your background is so shattered you will never amount to anything. It is only what you allow that you become – no one has the power to put you in a position you do not want, unless you allow them. Even the devil does not have the power to destroy your life unless you allow him, by something as little as a thought. Remember, positive thinking can change your life.

Romans 12: 2: … *and do not be conformed to this world but be transformed by the renewing of your mind, that you may prove what is that good and acceptable will of God.*

The prodigal son came to his senses, but it took thought for that self-realisation. Your thought is in your soul and if your thought is corrupt then everything about you will be corrupt. If your soul is corrupt, you can't hear from your spirit because God speaks to us through the spirit, which will go through the soul to the flesh. You need to constantly renew your mind, which can be done through meditating on God's word. Search yourself: what is the enemy saying to you? What is the word of God saying to you? You are not that person the world is saying you are. If it is not in the word of God, then it is not you.

> Joshua 1: 8 *This book of the law shall not depart from your mouth. You shall meditate in it day and night that you may observe to do all that is written in it for then you will make your way prosperous and then you will have good success.*

When you take time out to meditate on God's word – 5 minutes, 10 minutes and so on – it is not about how long – you will be more intentional in your decision-making, more forgiving, a better character, and more self aware because your thought controls your feeling which in turn controls your actions. You will hear more from God because his word is his voice.

The Prostitute; The Evangelist

There is a story in the bible about a prostitute who became an evangelist. Jesus, on his way to Galilee, passed through Samaria. He was so thirsty that he went to a well, where he saw a woman who was fetching water. He asked her for a drink of water. The woman was shocked because Samaritans had no dealings with the Jews and Jesus was a Jew.

After much conversation, Jesus told her to call her husband. She replied that she had no husband and Jesus told the woman her life history: how she had been with five husbands and the one she was with was not her husband. The woman was surprised.

When she finally left Jesus, she went into the city to tell the men and anyone who cared to know about Jesus.

The full story can be found in John Chapter 4: 5 -30.

The Samaritan woman must have been someone who was looked down on because of her way of life. People might have perceived her as being inconsistent, loose, dirty and a sinner but, when she encountered Jesus, her life changed for the better.

Useless

Nothing is useless, no one is useless.

It is amazing how used plastic can be recycled and used to produce sheets, film, non-food containers, bricks and so on. This was something that was originally meant to be thrown away and abandoned in the bin; it was supposed to be rubbish, useless, since the content has been used. The container is no longer useful. Typical of human beings. They will use and abandon you when you are no longer relevant to them.

This useless plastic is used to produce something useful.

Nothing and no one is useless in the hands of the right person. "Useless will remain useless in the hands of the wrong person." As I said, in the beginning, the earth was shapeless, formless, void. It took God who could see the future from the beginning, to speak into it and command things to be in place.

Apostle Isaiah once preached "the message in the mess." The first time I heard that phrase it touched my heart; it is indeed true. I once told a young man there is strength in his weakness. I told him to totally surrender to the Lord and allow Him to rule over his life because I could see the Lord wanted to use him, though he felt he was a mess and could not be used, he did not know God wanted to use his weakness to showcase his grace.

Chapter Four

The Tongue

The tongue, though little, has incredible powers. We can use our tongue to bring blessings and life or curses and death. The saying 'sticks and stones can break my bones but words will never hurt me' is a big fat lie. The tongue can be the most difficult thing to control and leaves us with great regret if we use our words to hurt people.

Psalm 45: 1 b, says, *My tongue is the pen of a ready writer.*

This means life comes as a blank cheque – you have the capacity to write what you want to see, fill it up with what you want to experience. The tongue, though tiny, is capable of mighty things.

The power of life and death are in the tongue. You can kill with your tongue or you can make life with it. In life, don't underestimate anything. It said that you can't judge a book by its cover. The tongue may look small, but when used by the wrong person, it can cause calamity, disaster, and destruction, while with the right person it will build, create, heal, bless, empower and multiply.

David's Stone

There was a little boy called David. He was a shepherd boy: homely, handsome, caring, passionate about the things of God and his father and family. David had brothers who were soldiers. At that time, the Philistines and Israel were not on good terms.

The Philistines had a soldier who was a giant. That giant terrorised Israel day and night. No one could challenge him and he stood all day disrespecting, insulting, and abusing the Israelites and their God.

Goliath challenged the Israelites to choose their best men to fight him, saying that, if their chosen one/s killed him, Goliath, the Philistines would become Israel's slaves, but if he, Goliath, killed the Israelite men then all of Israel would become the Philistine's slaves. Saul, the king of Israel, and his soldiers were scared.

At this time, David was taking food to his brothers. When he saw Goliath, he was upset about how much pride Goliath had and how he was so comfortable insulting his God. He asked what would be given to anyone who killed this uncircumcised philistine, as he called him. He was told.

Everyone was scared for David, including King Saul. David encouraged them not to give up hope. But Saul told David he was too young and inexperienced and he, Saul, had been in this business before David was born. David insisted, and, since it was his decision, he was allowed but they tried to dress him in the garments of war to protect him. But David could not move because the helmet, belt and sword were too heavy and he was not used to them. He took everything off, and took up his shepherd staff, selected five smooth stones, put them into the pocket of his shepherd pack and, with his sling in his hand, approached Goliath.

Goliath the giant underestimated David. He laughed and mocked Israel all the more, and David told him: 'You come at me with sword and spear and battle axe. I come at you in the name of God of the Angel-Armies of Israel who you cursed and mock.'

The soldiers were watching and confused. Goliath tried to attack David, but missed. David reached into his pocket for a stone, slung it and hit the Philistine hard in the forehead, embedding the stone deeply. Goliath crashed face-down in the dirt, and died. (This story can be found in 1samuel 17.)

Little things: David selected five stones but he only used one. Even though Goliath was a giant, it took the little, inexperienced boy to bring him down. God is intentional and interested in everything that concerns us. He cares, He loves and guards us.

Jealously

God asked Moses, 'What do you have in your hand?'

Moses used a rod to part the Red Sea. Even though Moses was a stutterer, God still used him to deliver the children of Israel from slavery.

Joseph became second in command in Egypt, a foreign land, from prison to the throne because God used him to interpret Pharaoh's dreams.

Nothing is useless in the hand of God. Nothing is little. Everyone is important, and useful, and can be used no matter the state.

Two Coins

There is a story in the bible of a widow who gave all she had during the time of Jesus at the temple. People were giving offerings, both rich and poor, and Jesus was observing. He noticed a woman who put in two small coins (like two cents) and Jesus called his Disciples and told them the widow gave more than everyone. They were surprised why he said that. He further told them what others gave was from the abundance of what they had, but she had given all she had. She gave what she could not afford; she gave her all. (Mark 12 : 41 to 44)

This woman was a widow – she had no husband, and therefore no support. She had nothing to fall back on – in effect, she gave her blood.

God does not overlook little things we do for him. He rewards us regardless; the motive of our action speaks volumes. Humans may see it as nothing; they can't see beyond that thing but God sees above and beyond what we do. He sees the seed that will be born from our actions. When you speak encouraging words to someone or you do things for someone, it goes beyond that moment.

While attending a church service, the pastor told a man that God had remembered him, that a financial blessing was coming to him because a few years ago, when he was a teenager, he gave someone who needed help a hundred dollars. Because of that, he was due for a financial reward. The man had even forgotten the act.

That is how far our acts of kindness can go. It goes into the future and provokes blessings, not just for us but also for our generation. Therefore, do not take anything for granted. No action or word is small; they are all capable of growth which can be positive or negative.

The Bread

How would you feel if someone threw bread at you and you fell, and never rise again? Isn't that strange? That sounds strange to me because bread is not strong; bread is weak, especially when you put it in water: it melts – it cannot survive pressure. So how can this weak thing or food be capable of killing someone?

Hmm. That is exactly what happened to the Midianites. This is the story of Gideon in the bible. He was a weak man, as he said. An angel of God appeared to him and told him he was to deliver the Israelites from the Midianite. The Midianites had oppressed Israel for seven years because Israel had sinned against God. God allowed their enemy to overpower them.

Gideon complained that he was not fit, strong, or ready for the assignment. He was not qualified. But God wanted to use his weakness to showcase his strength. When Gideon finally allowed God to use him for the battle, he went with a large number of men, but God told him the men were too many because the victory of Israel would not be by their strength. The men were finally reduced to the barest minimum but Gideon was still not confident ... until a man from his enemy's camp explained the dream he'd had concerning a loaf of bread that tumbled into the Midian camp. It came to the tent and hit it so hard the tent collapsed, then fell. The interpretation of the dream was that God would use Gideon to deliver the Israelites from their enemy.

The dream and its interpretation strengthened Gideon, and he and his men attacked the Midianites and overpowered them. (Judges 7)

When we don't know who we are and the power we possess, it does not stop us from having an encounter with God, and it does not stop him from using us. The bible says why we were yet sinners, Christ died for us. Even when we did not know we were sinners, he still chose us to be called his own. There is greatness within everyone; it takes the right words and actions to bring it out, like Gideon. He did not know who he was and what he could do. The right words from his enemy brought out the greatness within him.

I pray for anyone reading this book that you will discover the greatness within you and you will be strengthened for exploit in Jesus' name.

Tina

This might sound funny but I do appreciate little things people do for me, and I see and notice what people will not see or notice.

One day I was coming back from a night shift and my husband was going to work that morning. We had little kids we could not leave alone and we needed help. We needed someone to watch the kids for an hour before I arrived home. Someone was available and ready to help.

When I reached home, I saw her on the floor cleaning the tiles one after another. That touched my heart. For just an hour, she was helping me clean the house. When I got in, I told her not to worry but she insisted and cleaned the entire floor – it was sparkling clean.

The way Tina concentrated, focused, and applied herself to the cleaning really touched me. I find it worthy to mention it in this book because that made me love her more and I kept talking about it for months. To some, it may be nothing, but to me it was a big deal. For me, people have done both big and small things that I really appreciate. Nothing is small. Everything is big because the motive, effect, or outcome really counts.

Chapter Five

Daily Prayers

1.

1 Thessalonia 5:18. – *Thank you lord for today, thank you for your faithfulness, goodness, love and protection over my life and family.*

2.

Micah 7: 19. — Thank you lord for the blood of Jesus, the blood that speaks better things than the blood of Abel, thank you for the blood that speaks for me day and night. Thank you for throwing my sins in the depth of the sea. The blood of mercy, grace, love, peace, joy that speaks for me daily, am grateful lord.

3.

Romans 9: 15 to 16. Thank you for your mercy, Lord, you chose to show me mercy, am grateful, for you have shown mercy on whom you will have mercy and compassion on whom you will have compassion.

4. Thank the Lord for all he has been doing for you.

5.

2 Timothy 1:12. Lord I commit my day into your hand for I trust you are able to keep and Guard.

6.

Job 38:12 to 13. My day is blessed, I cover today with the blood of Jesus, I take charge of my day, I decree that today will favour me, I will work in goodness, and prosperity. My path will shine brighter and brighter, all things will align for me, good news is my portion, I will not struggle over anything in Jesus' name.

7.

1 King 10: 4 to 10. *The glory of the Lord will radiate through me, everything about me will reflect your goodness.*

8. I receive the direction and wisdom I need to exploit. I enjoy the benefit of today, whatever you have destined for me today will not pass me by.

9.

Mathew 18:18. *I bind every and any power that has been assigned against me today by the authority in the name of Jesus.*

10.

Jeremiah 1 : 10 I remove, pull down, destroy, shuck off, overthrow from the atmosphere whatever the enemies have spoken or done against me, from the North, South, East and West, you will not work, you will not stand in Jesus' name.

11.

Genesis 1:28 No power will stop my manifestation and my blessings today, the lord has given me dominion. I am in charge.

12.

Isaiah 54:17. *No weapon formed against me today will prosper and I condemn every evil tongue that has risen and will rise against me today.*

13.

Psalm 91: 7. *A thousand may fall at my side and ten thousand at my right hand but it shall not come near me in Jesus' name for I know you will give your Angels charge over me.*

14.

Job 1: 10. *I surround myself with a hedge of fire, no power of darkness will penetrate.*

15.

Psalm 1: 3. *Today I will bear good fruit, no matter what is happening in the world, my leaf will not wither and whatever I do shall prosper, when the world says there is a casting down, I will continue to say there is a lifting for my hope and trust is in you.*

About the Author

Olamma Maji is a graduate of Mass Communication; has a diploma in community service; is a pastor and author. She is a presenter of dgistwitholamma, as well as being a wife and a mother of four.

www.ingramcontent.com/pod-product-compliance
Lightning Source LLC
Chambersburg PA
CBHW030104100526
44591CB00008B/265